# YOU ARE GOD'S BEST

A CLASSIC
ON
HUMAN
VALUE

# BOOKS BY THE OSBORNS

**BELIEVERS IN ACTION**—*Apostolic–Rejuvenating*

**BIBLICAL HEALING**—*Seven Miracle Keys*
*4 Visions–60+ yrs. of Proof–324 Merged Bible Vs.*

**FIVE CHOICES FOR WOMEN WHO WIN**
*21st Century Options*

**GOD'S BIG PICTURE**—*An Impelling Gospel Classic*

**GOD'S LOVE PLAN**—*The Awesome Discovery*

**HEALING THE SICK**—*A Living Classic*

**JESUS & WOMEN**—*Big Questions Answered*

**LIFE–TRIUMPH OVER TRAGEDY (WHY)**
*A True Story of Life After Death*

**MIRACLES-PROOF of God's Love**

**NEW LIFE FOR WOMEN**—*Reality Refocused*

**NEW MIRACLE LIFE NOW**—*For Asia and The World*
*A Global Communiqué of The Christian Faith*

**PEACE IS A LIFESTYLE**—*Truths for Crisis Times*

**SOULWINNING**—*Outside The Sanctuary*
*A Classic on Biblical Christianity & Human Dignity*

**THE BEST OF LIFE**—*Seven Energizing Dynamics*

**THE GOOD LIFE**—*A Mini-Bible School–1,467 Ref.*

**THE GOSPEL ACCORDING TO T.L. & DAISY**
*Their Life & World Ministry–510 pg. Pictorial*

**THE MESSAGE THAT WORKS**
*T.L.'s Revealing Manifesto on Biblical Faith*

**THE POWER OF POSITIVE DESIRE**
*An Invigorating Faith Perspective*

**THE WOMAN BELIEVER**—*Awareness of God's Design*

**WOMAN WITHOUT LIMITS**
*Unmuzzled—Unfettered—Unimpeded*

**WOMEN & SELF-ESTEEM**—*Divine Royalty Unrestrained*

**YOU ARE GOD'S BEST**—*Transforming Life Discoveries*

**OSBORN**
**Ministries**
**International**

**USA HQ:**
*OSBORN MINISTRIES, INT'L*
P.O. Box 10, Tulsa, OK 74102 USA

T.L. OSBORN, FOUNDER
LaDONNA OSBORN, CEO

Tel: 918/743-6231
Fax: 918/749-0339    E-Mail: ministry@osborn.org
www.osborn.org

Canada: Box 281, Adelaide St. Post Sta., Toronto  M5C 2J4
England: Box 148, Birmingham  B3 2LG
(A Registered Charity)

BIBLE QUOTATIONS IN THIS BOOK MAY BE PERSONALIZED, PARAPHRASED, ABRIDGED OR CONFORMED TO THE *PERSON* AND *TENSE* OF THEIR CONTEXT IN ORDER TO FOSTER CLARITY AND INDIVIDUAL APPLICATION. VARIOUS LANGUAGE TRANSLATIONS AND VERSIONS HAVE BEEN CONSIDERED. BIBLICAL REFERENCES ENABLE THE READER TO COMPARE THE PASSAGES WITH HIS OR HER OWN BIBLE.

THE AUTHOR

ISBN 0-87943-134-2
Copyright 2003 by LaDonna C. Osborn
Printed in USA  2011-05
All Rights Reserved

# CONTENTS

# DEDICATED

To THE PARTNERS of our world ministry whose faithful support has enabled us to tell millions of people in nearly 100 nations that God values them, that He is not mad at them, and that the price He has paid for them is the proof of their worth.

T.L. Osborn

LaDonna, Osborn daughter

# INTRODUCTION

## God's Plan For You Is All Good

MARK TWAIN SAID, "Keep away from people who try to belittle your ambitions. Small people always do that. But really great people make you feel that you, too, can become great."

This statement expresses my father's belief. He has written this book to help you discover that YOU ARE GOD'S BEST. There is a sense of destiny in your life because you are God's idea, His dream.

Mary Crowley, a renowned Dallas business-woman said, "You are somebody because God never wastes His time to make a nobody."

We are convinced that the number one crisis in each human person centers on the question of his or her identity.

Have you considered these five basics for success?

1. Discover your RELATIONSHIP.

2. Assume your AUTHORITY.

3. Use your POWER.

4. Assess your WEALTH.

5. Believe in your DESTINY.

The concept that you have of yourself, of your value, of your purpose in life is the very core of what influences your personality.

A great psychologist said, "It is no exaggeration to say that a strong self-image is the best possible preparation for success in life."

This book will help you discover your roots in God:

* The value He places on you.

* The limitless potential within you.

* The vital principles of peace, prosperity, success and fulfillment He provides for you.

It is a positive book. It will help you and inspire you by encouraging you to discover your rich heritage and possibilities, with God at work in you.

This book is based on the Good News of the Bible. The news here is GOOD. God's plan for you is all GOOD. He is not mad at you. He loves you like you are and has already paid for every wrong you ever committed. That is what He wants you to know. He believes in you so much that He thinks you will respond positively to Him, as soon as someone tells you about His love plan.

# The French Prince

The story of the French prince who refused to curse, always inspires me. His father, King Louis XVI was beheaded, along with the queen, during the French Revolution.

When they prepared to guillotine the little prince, the crowd yelled, "Don't kill him. He is so young that his soul will go to heaven and that is too good for a member of this wicked royal family."

They announced their scheme:

"Give the prince to the witch. She will teach him to curse. Then he will sin, and when he dies, he will go to hell."

For months the witch tried in vain to force the prince to curse. He would stomp his feet and refuse, asserting, "I was born to be a king and I shall never speak that way."

When you discover what you were born for and the value that God places on you, it will affect your whole lifestyle. Your heritage is too great and your life is too important to ever be compromised.

To cower or fear or crawl in inferiority is to negate God's ideal for you in this life.

A Black man in the old South was told that he must accept his inferiority and learn to live with it. But he asked, "How can I be inferior, when I am a child of God?"

## Identity for Greatness

Through this book, my father will help you to make the greatest discovery you can ever make — your identity with God.

Realize that He never planned a failure, He designed you for success and happiness. He is not mad at you but He has paid an infinite price to redeem you to the position of His original dream for you.

When you realize these facts, you discover the doorway to abundant living.

This book is only GOOD news.

There is no condemnation in it. Jesus did not come to condemn anyone. Neither do we.

*God sent not his Son into the world to condemn the world; but that the world through him might be saved.*
Jn.3:17

The most unregenerate person deserves respect as a creation of God. No good is accomplished by criticizing, finding fault in or by belittling another human person.

Knowing that God invested so much to create humanity, then paid such a price to redeem each human being, we realize how much He values each person. This gives us reason to value them too.

## First Class All the Way

This book will lift you because it is based on GOOD news. My father and I never preach, teach or write in a way to demean, degrade, debase, discredit, depreciate, dishonor or disparage any human person for whom God has invested so much to restore to dignity.

Every human being deserves our highest respect and most sincere esteem as one for whom Jesus Christ laid down His life in love.

YOU ARE GOD'S BEST because He is first class all the way. He has created no second class human person. No one in God's family is inferior, insignificant, subordinate or subservient.

*The same Lord over all is rich to all that call on him. For whoever shall call on the name of the Lord shall be saved.* Rom.10:12-13

*For you are all the children of God. There is neither Jew nor Greek, there is neither bond nor free, there is neither male nor female: for you are all one.* Gal.3:26,28

LaDonna Osborn, D.Min.
CEO, Osborn Ministries International

---

LaDonna Osborn earned a Bachelor of Arts (BA) Degree from *Oklahoma City University*, a Master of Arts (MA) Degree in Practical Theology from *Oral Roberts University*, and a Doctor of Ministry (D.Min.) Degree from *American Christian College and Seminary*. She was awarded the honorary Doctor of Divinity Degree (DD) from both *Bethel Christian College* and *Zoe University*, and the Doctor of Humane Letters Degree (HLD) from the *Wesley Synod*.

I AM CREATED in God's likeness.

I am important in God's eyes.

He believes in me and He trusts me.

He loves me and He needs me as much as He loves or needs anyone else on earth.

He paid as much for me as He paid for any other human person who ever lived. )))➡

# Chapter I

# Created Like God

A YOUNG LADY in Europe ran away from home and traveled across the ocean to Tulsa, Oklahoma, just to talk to Daisy, my wife, and me.

From childhood, her parents had told her she was stupid, that she could not learn, that she was unattractive, that she could never get a job, that she could never attract a husband.

The more her parents said those things, the more they were engraved in her subconscious, and the more she acted out the part.

## Slavery of Negativism

This lady had always lived at home where she was dominated by a negative, destructive atmosphere. She became insecure, timid, withdrawn, and subjected.

Her father and mother had succeeded in making a slave of their own daughter — simply by planting negative, destructive seeds in her mind.

She was afraid to go out on the street alone. The only work she ever did was scrubbing floors.

Had she been as stupid as her parents told her she was, she could never have pondered a trip to America — to see T.L. and Daisy Osborn. She had to secretly get her own passport and visa and arrange for her ticket.

She was not dull witted or unintelligent. She was just emotionally starved. She had been mentally devastated by cruel parents who were transferring their own self-hatred to the closest victim they could reach — their own daughter.

## What You Talk Is What You Produce

Whether your words are positive or negative, they are seeds. They will produce, in your listeners, the type of people that you yourself are. Your words are your seeds and they engender, in people, the character of whatever you speak.

If you form the habit of talking about judgment and condemnation, you will produce those who judge and condemn you.

If you pronounce criticism toward others, you will harvest the kind of people who will rise and criticize you.

Whatever you sow in the minds of your listeners and in the minds of your family, you will personally reap. It is impossible to negate that law.

## Love Power in Action

We took that young European lady into our private prayer chamber, and showed her love, esteem and compassion. We could see that behind her emotionally scarred face was a brilliant, lovely lady who wanted to be somebody in life. She was extremely perceptive. She grabbed statements that lifted her self-esteem like a drowning person grabs a rope.

Her mouth and face twitched and grimaced uncontrollably as she talked. Her head and shoulders twisted involuntarily. Her whole body reflected her emotional state.

Almost anyone would have judged her unbalanced, yet her only problem was the ugly negative words and thoughts that had been heaped upon her by her own parents, in her own home.

## The New Confession

That young woman stood in our prayer room looking up to God. As tears rolled down her cheeks, I asked her to confess these things out loud:

**I am created in God's likeness. I am somebody important in God's eyes. He believes in me. He loves me and needs me. I am part of His plan. God loves me as much as He loves anyone else.**

Then we prayed with her, and when she returned to Europe, she was a new woman. She believed that she had a purpose for living, that she could succeed in life, that God was vitally interested in her and that He valued her.

She was thinking positive thoughts about herself, walking more uprightly, with her shoulders straight. She could smile. She had hope. She believed that God had a plan for her. She had a new outlook. Her whole life would change because her thoughts were changed.

## The Battered Beaten Penny

Just before she left, Daisy and I were on our forty-minute daily jogging course alongside the river in Tulsa, and I saw on the trail a battered, beaten penny. It was so scarred by the hundreds of vehicles that had rolled over it that you could hardly identify it.

I picked it up and as I held it in my hand, the Lord whispered to me: "That coin is worth as much as a beautiful, brand new, shining penny. Its value is the same. It is like that dear lady from Europe.

"Go tell her what I have said to you. Though she is scarred and battered by her parents and acquaintances, tell her she is as valuable as the most beautiful lady in Europe."

I took that coin and placed it in her hands and while she looked at it, I gave her God's message. Then while she held it, she repeated after me:

"My life is like this battered coin. But I am as valuable as the most perfect and beautiful person in Europe!"

She promised to keep that coin with her Bible. She purposed that every time anyone would say anything derogatory to her, she would hold that battered coin and say:

"My life is like this battered coin. But I am as valuable as the most perfect and beautiful person in Europe!"

The change that has taken place in her life has been miraculous.

## She Discovered God's Value

She discovered the facts that gave her self-esteem. She is God's creation. He loves her and paid a supreme price—the death of His own Son, to redeem her back to Him so that she and God could be at one again, could walk together again and could share life again as He originally planned for her.

That is what He planned for you, and it is He who caused me to write this book for you, so you can discover that YOU ARE GOD'S BEST.

I AM CREATED in the image of God, to be like Him, to manifest Him in human form.

I am made...

* For life and love.
* For power and prosperity.
* For success and progress.
* For dignity and divinity.　　　⟫⟫⟫

# Chapter 2

# Start Your Miracle

THE BASIC PRINCIPLE to be discovered in this book is so powerful that it will actually start the miracle you need in life.

God's power will begin working in you as you go through these pages. You will discover this great principle if you are alert to it in your heart.

Problems will be solved. Sicknesses will go away. Fear and apprehension will disappear. Guilt will be gone. Insecurity will vanish. You will begin rising up on the inside.

As you discover this powerful principle, accept it with intelligence. You are ready for it. That is why this book has come to you at this time. You can grasp any principle you are ready for.

## Read and Discover

The seeds that will be planted in you through this book will produce God's best in your life. They will work like a miracle.

You will be able to look at what was an impossibility and say, "Now I know what to do, what to say, how to deal with this and win."

## Destiny Is Now at Work in You

Why were you chosen for this information which has lifted tens of thousands of people around the world?

It is God's way of saying:

**"I love you. I created my best when I created you.** I paid a price for you and you are worth all I ever paid for you. I have destined my best for you."

As I share with you this vital, basic principle to success, peace and happy living, be like Thomas Edison. Someone asked him how he gave the world so many inventions. He said: "Because I never think in words, I think in pictures."

So try to just let your mind soar. Then dare to be a believer in all that God designed you for.

## To Begin, Say This

Right now, for a starter, decide to believe and accept the following facts about your life. Say to yourself:

**"I am created in the image of God, to be like Him,** to manifest Him in human form. I am made for life and love, for power and prosperity, for success and progress, for dignity and divinity."

As you respond to these facts and believe that

you have unique value and purpose, you are planting the seeds of truth in you which guarantee that this is the kind of harvest you will reap in life.

> **God made nothing inferior. He is first class all the way. He created you unique. You are exceptional, one of a kind.**

Before you were born, you existed in God's mind. He knew this world would need you at this time. He planned you with a special purpose that no one but you could fulfill because no one on earth could do what you are here to do.

## God Sees the Terrific You

This is a powerful fact.

God never planned for any one to become a waste, a non-achiever, a failure, or a casualty in life. No one was ever intended for prostitution or infidelity, for neglect or shame, for sickness or suffering, for destructiveness or non-productivity.

No human being was ever destined by God to crawl in shame or to cower in fear.

God looks at the terrific you He created you to be.

Jesus saw in Peter the unbeatable leader in the church which he was destined to become. He saw that quality in him while he was still an ordinary fisherman. It amazed Peter's contemporaries when Jesus called him *a stone.*[Jn.1:40-42]

Right now, you are getting a picture of the you God created and brought to this world for this particular time.

Can you accept yourself as being created in God's image, made to be like Him?

David said in Psalms 8:5, *God has made you a little lower than the angels* (original Hebrew: *a little lower than God).* Can you see yourself as a creature in God's class of being?

## The Dream That God Esteems

God has never given up on His esteem for you. You may be down on yourself, but God values you. You may condemn yourself or allow others to discredit you, but God will only lift you up.

We are His masterpieces, charged to rule and to have dominion over everything that He created on this earth.[Gen.1:28-30; Psa.8:6-8]

See yourself in God's image. Realize that you were never created to be poor, unhappy, dominated, manipulated, abused, shamed or walked on.

You are created in God's class of being, to walk and talk and live and reign with Him in life. He designed you for His abundance, for His nobility, for His kingdom. Nothing can stop or limit you, once you discover this vital principle.

# START YOUR MIRACLE

DISCOVER THE VALUE God places upon you.

Stop condemning yourself, then you can stop condemning others.

Start believing in what God has created you to be, then you can start believing in God's love plan for others. )))➤

# Chapter 3

# Discovering Dignity

Y OU ARE GOD'S BEST.

His plan is that you discover this fact. That is why this book is in your hands right now. God has you marked. You fit into His plan.

As you become aware of these facts, you will decide to stop your self-condemnation, your self-destruction. You will no longer beat yourself down with accusing, negative thoughts and confessions.

No one has the right to destroy or to disparage what God has created, in His own image, and has paid so much to redeem and to justify.

## God's Love Plan

Adam and Eve were created and placed in the Garden of Eden to walk and talk with God and to live with Him.

They were made in His own image, destined to plan and work with Him, carrying out His ideas on earth.[Gen.1:26-31]

Then temptation came.[Gen.3:1-6] Man and woman sinned and were driven out of God's presence, [Gen.3:22-24] to become the slaves of Satan whom they believed and obeyed. They forfeited their right to self-esteem, self-dignity and self-worth.

God, in His love, never abandoned His dream of having man and woman, whom He had created in His own image, near Him. But being righteous, He could not condone sin.[Isa.59:1-3]

His law could not be moderated. *The soul that sins shall die.*[Eze.18:4,20] All had sinned, so all would die. [Rom.5:12]

But one who was perfectly innocent could take the place of the guilty and die as their substitute. Since no crime could be punished twice, once the punishment was suffered by a willing and perfectly innocent substitute, the crime of the guilty would be paid for, and the guilty would be justified as though he or she had never sinned.[Rom.5:1]

Jesus Christ, God's Son, was perfect.[Heb.5:9] He had never sinned.[2Cor.5:21; Heb.4:15;7:26; 1Pet.1:19;2:22] He came to this world and took on himself the sins of the whole world and suffered our full penalty.[Jn. 1:29; 1Pet.2:24; 2Cor.5:21]

*God so loved the world that he gave his only begotten Son, that whoever believes in him should not perish but have everlasting life.*[Jn.3:16]

All that would ever be required of us to receive

total justification before God, is that we simply believe with all of our hearts that Jesus Christ died in our place, and respond to such love by willingly confessing to others what we believe.[Rom.10:9-10]

Once we comprehend the Good News of what Jesus did for us and once we believe it with our heart and confess it to others, an incredible miracle takes place:

> *God took the sinless Christ and poured into him our sins. Then, in exchange, he poured God's goodness into us.* [2Cor.5:21LB]

Jesus Christ became the way back to God for you and for me. Through His sacrifice:

* He removed forever the condemnation of our sins and dissolved the barrier between us and God, so that we are now welcome to return to His presence where we can once again share His lifestyle.[Heb.10:18-22]

* We have been restored to the dignity and righteousness of God for which He originally created us.

* We have been **justified**—as though we had never turned away from Him and had never sinned.

## Restored to God

Once we have understood that our sins separated us from God, but that God loved us too much to leave us to die in our sins; once we have believed that Jesus Christ died in our place, once we have repented of our sins and have accepted Jesus as our Savior and received Him and His life in us, we are regenerated, we are saved, we are redeemed.

When this miracle has come to pass, we are new creatures in Christ Jesus, and we must never again condemn, discredit or slander what God has paid so much to redeem and to justify.

The Bible clearly teaches that when we hear of God's love plan, we should come to Him in repentance, confess our sins to Him and confess that we accept His love plan; then He forgives us, receives us and imparts His power within us to make us His children again, and we become new creatures in Christ Jesus.[Ac.2:38]

But once we have accepted God's forgiveness and once we believe that the life of Jesus Christ has been imparted to us and has transformed us, we are not to go through life confessing that we are weak, rebellious, unworthy, sinning worms of the dust.

Once we have been converted:

* **We become sons and daughters of God.**[Jn.1:12]

* We belong to His family.

* We are recreated in His image.

* We are born again.

* We are hooked up with deity.

## Discover the New Life

The coming of Jesus Christ and the Good News has brought to us a new and positive message, of a new creation, a new birth, a new life, a new nature, a new way. *If you are in Christ, you are a new creature: old things are passed away; behold, all things are become new.*[2Cor.5:17]

The new birth is a miracle. When you come to Christ, you are made new. You are changed. Believe in that change. Think about that change. Confess it. Sing about it. Act like you have been changed.

When you stop condemning yourself, then you can stop condemning others. As you start believing in yourself, then you can believe in others.

## Seeing Yourself in Others

Out on the western plains of America a new immigrant family arrived in the town. They halted their wagon by a farmer's house and asked him: "What kind of people live around here?"

The old farmer said, "Well, newcomer, what kind of people lived in the old country where you came from?"

"Oh," the immigrant replied, "it was terrible. There were crooks and liars, deceivers and dishonest people everywhere. The businessmen were crooked and the officials were worse. That's why we left the place, to find a new world."

"Well," the farmer said, "I expect that is the kind of people you will find around here too."

The next day, another load of immigrants arrived and stopped to talk with the farmer. They too wanted to know what kind of people had settled in that area.

The wise old farmer asked, "Well, newcomer, what kind of people lived in the old country where you came from?"

"Oh," the immigrant replied, "it was a fine land. We had fine neighbors. Our merchants were honorable. Our people cared for each other. It was hard to leave them, but we thought we could bring some of our good out west and help to build this great new nation."

"Well, sir," said the farmer, "you are going to be mighty happy here. I think you will find that same kind of people out here."

We see in **others** what we see in **ourselves**. The person who does not trust others, is not a trustworthy person. If we believe we are bad, we will believe others are bad. If we suspicion dishonesty in others, it is a sign that we need to reexamine our own attitude.

## Discover These Facts

1. Discover that God created you to be like Him. Gen.1:27

32

2. Discover that when sin entered the human family through Adam and Eve,[Gen.3] God did not want you to die for your sins,[2Pet.3:9] though His law prescribed that *the wages of sin is death.* [Rom.6:23]

3. Discover that He loved you too much to let you die. [Jn.3:16] He gave His Son, Jesus Christ, to assume all of the legal punishment, judgment and condemnation for every sin you ever committed. [2Cor.5:21]

4. Discover that since Jesus suffered all the punishment for your sins and paid all of your debt when He died in your place on the cross, you were freed from all guilt and judgment,[Rom.8:32-33] because no crime can be judged twice and no debt can be paid twice.

5. Discover that God paid that supreme price for you to prove how much He values you and how much He wants to share His life with you. [Eph.2:13-16; Isa.53]

6. Discover that since your sins are punished and your debt is paid in full by the life and blood of Jesus Christ,[Rev.1:5] you are free, and no longer guilty — if you only believe that Christ died in your place. [Col.1:20-22; Rom.3:22; Psa.34:22]

7. Discover that since your sins are remitted forever [Ac.10:43; Mat.26:28] and since there is nothing to separate you from God,[Isa.59:12; Rom.8:38-39] now when you confess and receive Jesus Christ,[Rom.10:9-10] you are allowing God to come home to you — you and

He are able to walk together again [Eph.2:13] like Adam and Eve walked with God in the garden of Eden before they sinned against Him.[Gen.3:8]

8. Discover that through what Christ suffered on your account, there is nothing left for you to suffer; no judgment, no guilt, no condemnation. [Tit.3:5-7; Gal.2:16; Eph.2:8-9] You are **justified** before God.[Rom.5:1] A child said: "I am **just-as-if-I'd** never sinned!"

9. Discover that now, the moment you accept these facts in your heart and believe them and confess Jesus Christ as your personal Savior and Lord, you are saved, converted, redeemed, restored, made whole, uplifted, blessed, accepted, renewed, regenerated, reborn to the same kind of God life for which you were originally created.[Ac.2:21;4:12] All of that is what the Bible calls salvation.[1Th.5:9; 2Tim.2:10; Heb.5:9]

## Who You Are in Christ

Now you can understand why I say that when you discover who you really are in Christ, you will stop condemning yourself, and you will stop condemning others.

Knowing the price God paid to redeem you and to restore you to His lifestyle, you will no longer condemn what God has redeemed, or put down what God has paid so much to lift up.

In our great soulwinning institutes overseas, we gather thousands of Christians together and teach them for two hours, three times each day.

Do you know where we begin? We start by emphasizing these six facts of the new Christ life:

1. God is what He says He is.
2. I am what He says I am.
3. God has what He says He has.
4. I have what He says I have.
5. God will do what He says He will do.
6. I can do what He says I can do.

After we get people to accept those six fundamental facts, then we start at the new birth, and focus on the miracle transformation of our old nature to the new Jesus life.

## See the You That God Sees

We underscore the fact that we must see ourselves as God sees us. We must think of ourselves like God thinks of us, and confess what He says about us instead of what traditional theology says about us.

Each lesson we teach them is a challenge to new possibilities in the life of Christ. Never is there condemnation. Always there is faith, hope and love.

Wherever we define those principles, we lift

people. Multitudes of from 20,000 to 300,000 have swarmed our campaigns in over a hundred nations during more than six decades. We proclaim the Good News and we proclaim it glad — not mad.

The world has enough hate and prejudice without getting more from the pulpit or podium. Christ never came to condemn people, but to love and bless and save them.[Jn.3:17; Lu.19:10]

No one has the right to stand in a pulpit or before a class and fill the minds of people with negative, unpleasant phrases and pronouncements, and destroy their self-esteem and reverence for life with ugly, negative words and thoughts.

## Good News—Not Condemnation

Jesus condemned no one — not even the adulterous woman and man [Jn.8:11] or the thief on the cross.[Lu.23:43] And as His ambassadors,[2Cor.5:20] we do not either.

There is new life in Christ,[Jn.10:10; 1Jn.5:12] not condemnation.

There is salvation in Him,[Heb.5:9] not slavery to religion, not guilt.

There is deliverance in Him,[Lu.4:18] not captivity.

Our message does not wound but it heals. We represent Christ, we do not destroy. We give life and joy and peace.

The greatest challenge we have is to communicate the gospel of Jesus Christ to the unconverted without offending those already converted.

Christianity is not morbid and depressing.

It is the Good News that we have been redeemed.

Anyone can now rise and walk again with God.

The most irreligious and unbelieving person has unlimited possibilities in God.

Anyone can become a new creature in Christ.
2Cor.5:17

This is the doorway to a new kind of abundant living. That is the principle which God has led you to discover today.

## A New Beginning

A great Christian leader in America has edited many of the great old church hymns which they use in their church worship.

The self-condemning lines have been replaced by phrases of faith and new living. The struggling thoughts have been changed to thoughts of victory in Christ. The verses that pour out negativism now radiate positive attitudes. They keep the familiar music but change the words to lift, invigorate and inspire the congregation to have faith in God's plan for life.

Here are seven statements about you which I hope you will engrave in your mind, by rehearsing them until they become a part of you.

1. I am created in God's likeness.

2. I am unique — one of a kind.

3. I am of infinite value — to God and to others.

4. I am loved, in spite of my faults.

5. I am redeemed and accepted by the Lord.

6. I am empowered for His divine service to others.

7. I am commissioned as an ambassador in His royal kingdom.

# DISCOVERING DIGNITY

THE SEEDS OF greatness are in me.

God never created me to be a nobody, but a real somebody.

I shall never again discredit or demean or destroy what God created in His own image and values so much.　　　　　⟫⟫➡

# Chapter 4

# Energizing Power

AN INSANE MAN by the name of Kariuki was brought to one of our teaching meetings overseas. Many thousands of people were there.

Kariuki was known as the running maniac. His hair and beard were long, disheveled and flea-infested. His body was filthy. His rags barely covered his nakedness.

He ran across the hills of Kikuyuland for seventeen years, practically nude, demented, clutching rubbish in his arms, running from one village to another, throwing the worthless stuff down and desperately gathering more bits and pieces, as though he must cling to something.

God never created anybody to be unable to think and act normally, nor to live in shame and disgrace.

A young preacher had reached out to Kariuki in the kind of love that sends a person out to share Christ with others. He conceived a way to entice him into his little pickup so he could bring him to the crusade.

I did not know that such an insane man was in the audience that day as I planted the seeds of human value in the minds of the people.

## The Miracle Power of Truth

There is a miraculous power in truth. I believe words are seeds. They have the ability to produce what they say. They are energizers.

I believe that God's words are energized by His own divine, miracle working life. He created the world by the power of His word, and the Bible says, *the word of the Lord endures forever.*[1Pet.1:25] His word is as powerful today when we speak or teach or announce it, as it ever was. That is what we believe when we stand before the multitudes to teach the powerful and positive gospel of Jesus Christ.

The day Kariuki was brought to our crusade in Nyeri, Kenya, I was teaching the people about being created in God's image, about His original design and plan for each human being, about His love for us even though we had sinned, about the price Jesus Christ paid to redeem us to God, about how to believe the gospel and to accept Jesus as Savior.

I emphasized the value of each human person.

I said to the multitude:

**"Each one of you is beautifully and wonderfully made in God's image. Every individual**

among you is special. You do not have to be second class. You are each unique. God who created you like Himself, put you here for a purpose so special that no one else on earth can do what you are here to do."

Those word-seeds had power.

There is a remarkable statement in the Bible about the power of Jesus' words.

*As he was teaching, the power of the Lord was there to heal the people.*[Lu.5:17]

That has to be what happened to Kariuki who was brought to our meeting that day.

## Everybody Is a Real Somebody

We taught that crowd the essence of what I am sharing with you in this book. We emphasized that God made no one for failure, poverty, sickness or shame; that everybody is a real somebody in God's eyes.

I urged that audience to personally accept the fact that each of you are a special creation of God and to begin believing that by cooperating with God, you can discover new life through believing on Jesus Christ and through accepting Him by faith.

In some miraculous way those seeds of truth penetrated Kariuki and his mind was healed and his life was transformed in one glorious moment when God's loving compassion and power restored him to his right mind by a miracle.

Kariuki had stood by the side of the man who had brought him to the meeting, clutching his armful of rubbish. We had preached, not knowing anything about such an insane man being present.

## The Healing Power of God's Word

Almost all of the great miracles that we have witnessed during over six decades of mass miracle evangelism in more than a hundred nations—and we may have seen as many or more than any others have ever been privileged to see—almost all of them have taken place out in the crowd, while we were teaching the people or praying for them, without us knowing anything about the case until the miracle had already taken place.

Kariuki was out there listening that day as we preached and prayed. The Spirit of the Lord that bathed that great field of people in His love came upon Kariuki in some way that I cannot explain. In a moment, the demons were gone from him. He was well. He was normal.

He asked the man who brought him, "What am I doing with this stuff in my arms?"

The young preacher diplomatically helped him to get rid of it.

Then he realized that Kariuki was really healed.

He brought him to the platform so the audience could know about the wonder God had done.

There Kariuki stood. His clothes were so torn and dirty that they scarcely covered his nudity. He looked wild. His hair was long and matted. It was full of fleas. His beard was long. His body emitted a terrible odor.

But when I looked into his eyes, I could see that this man had been visited by the Lord. It was obvious.

I took him by the shoulders and as I looked at him, I said, "Kariuki, you look beautiful." That lifted him.

## Good Seeds Grow Good Crops

I said, "Kariuki, you are my brother. Did you know, my father and your father is the same? We are one." And I pulled him to me and embraced him, then leaning back, I looked at him again.

I said, "Kariuki, I am so proud of you. You are going to go places. God my father made you. He has a plan for you that nobody in the world can carry out as good as you can." Then I embraced him again.

Then he gave a beautiful testimony about the horror of his seventeen years as a demented maniac, of how Jesus came to him and healed him while I was teaching the gospel, and of how wonderful and peaceful it was to be free from that terrible mental oppression that had destroyed his life for so many years.

When he had finished talking, I told the preachers, "Take him and bathe him. Disinfect him. Give him a haircut. Trim his beard. Buy him new shoes and new clothes. Get a beautiful necktie. Get him a Bible. Bring him back tomorrow. I want the multitude to see what God has done."

The next day, Kariuki was sitting on the platform. You would have thought he was one of the preachers. In fact, he always sat on the platform during each meeting for the rest of the crusade. He never missed a night.

Every evening I asked him to read the scripture lesson for me before I began to teach. As he read the scriptures the entire community would marvel again at the miracle God had done in their city. Every one knew the crazy, running maniac. Now they were overwhelmed as they saw him, each day, sane, normal, well and happy.

In Bible days, *many believed on his name, when they saw the miracles which he did.*[Jn.2:23] *And a great multitude followed him, because they saw the miracles which he did on them that were diseased.*[Jn.6:2]

It was the same in Nyeri. Thousands turned to the Lord because they saw the wonderful miracles which Christ did through the power of the gospel.

Kariuki was perfectly normal. He was clean, groomed and wore his suit each day. He attended every meeting, listening, learning and developing into a remarkably balanced gentleman.

## Start Your Own Miracle Now

The power of the truths I am sharing with you in this book, brought him all the way from a running, half naked, wild man to a groomed, well dressed Christian gentleman. He found good employment and has become a positive influence in the Kikuyu community. His is a living example of one who rose from emptiness to meaningful living and discovered his own personal value as a marvelous creation of God.

I AM VALUABLE because I am created in God's class of being.

I am vital because God's plan involves me.

))))➤

# Chapter 5

# You Are Valuable As You Are

A DRUNKARD, lying in a gutter clutching his bottle, was attracted by a Christian who was sharing the gospel on the street.

The preacher emphasized the importance of life and was trying to help people realize their own value as persons created in God's likeness.

He stressed the price God had paid for the salvation of each individual; that He loved us so much that He paid for our redemption by giving His own Son, Jesus Christ, to die in our place.

The drunkard was touched by the idea that God valued him that much. It had never occurred to him that his life had value to God.

## God Values People Like They Are

When the street preacher concluded his talk, the drunk man called out: "Sir, I want to be saved. But I am drunk. I am no good."

The preacher said, "Friend, God loves you like you are. He created you like Himself. He has already paid to redeem you. He holds nothing against you if you believe Jesus Christ died in your place. He values you just like you are. Jesus has paid for your salvation. Just accept Him and His love for you."

"I do. I do," the drunk man said in tears.

And he was transformed.

In his drunken state, Jesus came to his life and saved and changed him. His bottle had no more appeal. He became a follower of Christ and was restored to a productive life.

## See Yourself As God Sees You

The miracle began when he realized that he was valuable to God.

When you accept your own self-value, you can accept God's value of others.

When you realize how God esteems you, how He created you in His own image, then you can accept the fact that you, as one of God's offspring, deserve happiness, peace, success and fulfillment in life.

Nobody on earth can ever make you feel inferior, unworthy or undeserving again.

## Bartender, the Drinks Are on Me

A personal friend of mine who is the pastor of a large, soulwinning church on the West Coast, was converted and called to preach the gospel while drinking at a bar in a nightclub.

He was thinking about God's love for him and how God valued him just like he was. God's Spirit suddenly visited him as he was standing at the bar. He decided to stop destroying what God had paid so much to save.

He bowed his head and prayed, confessing his sins and accepted Jesus Christ and His love right there in the nightclub.

Leaning on the bar, he wept aloud and received Jesus as His Lord. As he wept, he told the Lord he would give his life to tell others about His love and miracle power.

Then he raised his head, and when he did, he said that dingy nightclub looked like a bit of heaven to him.

His joy and peace were so intense that he wanted to celebrate his conversion, so in a spontaneous outcry to the others in the bar, he yelled:

"Listen, everybody. Jesus Christ has saved me right here today. And I have promised Him to give my life to telling people about His love and power.

"This calls for a celebration. Everybody come on. Bartender, set 'em up. The drinks are on me."

## The Unorthodox New Beginning

I agree, that was pretty unorthodox but the man

was sincere, and from that day, which terminated his life of drinking and carousing, he began his training for the ministry and has become an outstanding and successful pastor and Christian leader.

When you discover that God values you, and that He has paid a supreme price for you because He loves you, you discover the principle that opens the gateway to true happiness, peace, success and fulfillment in life.

# YOU ARE VALUABLE AS YOU ARE

J ESUS SAID, "Behold my hands. I am Jesus."

The Hindu saw the proof of how much God valued him.

The price that was paid for me is evidence of what I am worth to God. ⟫➤

# Chapter 6

# Love Proved Your Value

IT IS WONDERFUL when you get God's viewpoint, His attitude about you and your life.

Here is some of what God says about us in the New Testament:

*So now we have been made right in God's sight because of what Jesus Christ our Lord has done for us.*

*He has brought us into this place of highest privilege where we now stand, and we confidently and joyfully look forward to actually becoming all that God has had in mind for us to be.*

*We are able to hold our heads high, for we know how dearly God loves us.*

*Now we rejoice in our wonderful new relationship with God—all because of what our Lord Jesus Christ has done in dying for our sins making us friends of God.* Rom.5:1,2,5,11LB

Remember these three statements:

* He has brought us to this place of highest privilege.

* We joyfully look forward to becoming all that God has in mind for us to be.

* We rejoice in our wonderful new relationship —making us friends of God.

## How God Valued a Villager

A dear village man who had a terrible rupture, and one lame leg, attended one of our crusades. The first night he came, he learned how God valued him so much that He gave His Son to redeem him. He believed the message and Jesus completely and instantly healed him.

The next night he carried his daughter to the crusade. She had been crippled from polio and could not walk. As she heard the gospel, she too believed on the Lord and was saved. Then she was miraculously healed as her father had been. She could walk, run and jump as well as anyone.

Then the old man brought his insane sister. She had to be kept chained to a tree like a wild animal because she was totally deranged and physically dangerous.

Four men helped bring her to the crusade. They helped hold her and keep her quiet during the meeting. As we taught, *the power of the Lord was present to heal.*[Lu.5:17] The evil spirits which had taken control of her mind went out of her and she was completely healed and restored by the power and the presence of Christ.

These remarkable miracles came to pass in this family through faith in God's word of promise. They discovered that God valued them and paid a price to redeem them to Him. He loved them and wanted to come and live with them.

## The Principle of God's Value

This is the message that gave that father faith in God. No one ever told him that he, a poor African villager, was valuable to God, that his paralyzed, helpless daughter was vital to God's plan, that his demented sister, foaming at the mouth and shrieking like a wild animal, was so valuable to God that He had paid for her to be restored to His lifestyle.

This is the principle that opened the door to a new and powerful faith in Christ and His love. That African villager received faith through discovering these truths as we taught them. That discovery enabled him to call on the Lord with faith, and his entire family was blessed and restored to peace with God and to new vibrant physical health.

As you discover the principle of your value to God and of His intense love for you, then you can call on Him in faith and the miracle you need will be done.

## Behold My Hands! I Am Jesus!

In one of our crusades in India a young, arrogant, university student stood at the back of the crowd with folded arms, seething in anger. He wondered what he could do to drive these foreign teachers out of his town and to stop our influence on his people.

But as we preached about Jesus and then prayed, suddenly the Lord appeared to that young political activist. As Jesus looked straight into the young man's eyes, He opened His nail-pierced hands and said, "*Behold my hands! I am Jesus!*" Then with a soft smile and eyes of compassion, He disappeared.

The young man fell to his knees weeping and received Jesus Christ as his Lord and master. He told the whole multitude what had happened to him and hundreds accepted the Lord.

That man saw the Lord and his life was changed forever. He realized the price God had paid to prove how He valued him.

We have preached before multitudes in over a hundred nations and I know something of the doctrines and teachings of the world's great religious founders — Mohammed, Buddha, Confucius and others.

* Jesus Christ is the **only** one who died for His followers.

* He is the **only** one who loved them enough to lay down His life for them.

* He is the **only** one who rose from the dead and

came back to live and carry on His ministry of love in and through those who believe on Him.

When He returned from the grave, He did not lecture them about His suffering and love for them.

He just showed them His hands and His side. He showed them the nailprints and the wound of the sword that was thrust through His body.

## Nailprints Proved His Love

His message was: *Peace be to you. Behold my hands and my feet, that it is I myself. He showed them his hands and his feet.*Lu.24:36,39-40

That is what He did to that young Hindu in our meeting in India. He opened His hands and said: "Behold my hands. I am Jesus."

The nailprints were the **proof** of His love.

Jesus Christ is the only one who has nailprints in His hands. Confucius or Mohammed or Buddha do not have them. Jesus bears the eternal scars which prove how much God thinks you and I are worth.

That is the principle of truth which opens the door to your new life with God. He values you. If you ever question it, remember His scars—the proof of the value He places on you today, just like you are. He loves you.

He proved it. You can trust His love.

IF THAT IS the me God sees in me,
then that is the me that I shall be.

It is right that I esteem what God esteems
and that I value what He values.

I accept the value God has placed on me.

))))➤

# Chapter 7

# True Self-Esteem

CREATED IN GOD'S IMAGE, you are His kind of being.

An artist was attracted by a beggar who sat across the pathway. Thinking of God's handiwork in every human being, the perceptive artist painted the man as he imagined him to potentially become. Then he called the beggar to see the painting.

"Is that me?" the beggar asked.

"That is the you I see in you!" replied the artist.

"If that is the man you see in me," the beggar stated with new purpose in his eyes, "then that is the man that I shall be!"

## Esteem What God Esteems

Your God-given value does not depend on special genes from superior parents. Your worth before God is not measured by your assets, the color of your skin, super intelligence or formal education.

Created by God, you are His offspring.

It is right that you esteem what God esteems and value what God values.

All sorts of miracles start happening when you discover and accept your value and your potential.

The Bible says, *You are God's workmanship.*[Eph.2:10]

## Made in God's Image

The man who wrote most of the Psalms was awestruck by how God made human persons.

*The Lord made people a little lower than God* [Original Hebrew — God; King James Version — angels] *and crowned them with glory and honor. You have given them dominion over the works of your hands; you have put all things under their feet.*[Psa.8:5-6]

The bottom line of positive and stable self-esteem is when you can say:

## "I accept the value that God has put on me."

When you do that, you will then cooperate with God to develop the best possible you in this world.

## The Worth of Self-Value

**Self-value** will rid you of all jealousy because you will never again want to be anyone else.

**Self-value** will wipe out inferiority because you are in God's class of being and He, in you, is greater than any person or any power outside of you.[1Jn.4:4]

**Self-value** will eliminate fear of failure or defeat because nothing can stop you and God working together.

**Self-value** will give you courage because you discover that with God at work in you, you become indomitable.

**Self-value** will cause you to stand up tall, to square your shoulders, to look out into the future with new confidence, to walk with a steady stride, and to rise to the level of the importance for which God created you.

I AM BEAUTIFUL.

God has a plan for me that no one else on earth can do as well as I can.

He believes in me and He trusts me.

I am a member of royalty.

No one can ever stop God and me together.

We are people lifters.　　　　　　⟫➤

# Chapter 8

# Loved, Like You Are

YOU ARE SOMEBODY. You are loved and you are important. God believes in you. You are part of His plan. You are unique, the only one of you that God has.

Say it and think it, pray it and sing it until you actually believe it. When you do, you will be dynamite.

How fortunate it would be if every person who is born again could hear those facts just as soon as the salvation miracle took place.

The words and ideas planted in a child's mind during the first four or five years of its life, are what form the lifestyle and attitude of that child all of its life.

## Seeding the New Believer

When the insane man, Kariuki, was healed and born again in our Nyeri crusade, the first words He heard were:

"Kariuki, you are beautiful. You are valuable to

God and to people. God has a plan for you that no one else on earth can do as well as you. God's plan depends on you. You are my brother. My father is your father. God paid as much for you as He did for me. You are terrific, Kariuki. You are a member of God's family. God is with you. You are destined for success. No one can ever beat you and God together. Kariuki, you are loved. You are wonderful."

Those words formed Kariuki's life. He went right out and began sharing Christ with people. He was employed. He became productive. He loved people. He witnessed of Christ to them. He believed in his importance to God. He believed in success. He was a winner from the beginning of his new life with Christ.

No one said, "Now Kariuki, be careful. You are only a sinner saved by grace. You are an unworthy worm of the dust. You must be careful or you will fall into temptations and lose your salvation. You must remember, the devil is strong and he will deceive you. God will test you and be out to get you if you sin. He will bring calamity upon you to judge you. You are unworthy. You are weak. You are only a baby in Christ. You must stay lowly and expect problems to teach you humility."

He believed Jesus had come to live in him and to minister and witness through him. He believed Jesus was His only Lord and master. He believed

God valued and loved him. He believed he was important to God.

Kariuki's life became a lift to people as he reached out to love and help others to know Christ who had paid for his recovery.

## Valued in God's Plan

God paid a supreme price for you too—the blood and life of His only begotten Son, Jesus Christ.

He would not pay that price for a **nobody.** He would only pay such a price for a **somebody.**

You may have considered yourself unworthy of God's blessings, due to your past life.

But remember: Jesus Christ died to save people who are sinners.

God's pardon is only offered to those who have done wrong.

God's redemption is only for those who are lost.

Jesus welcomes you and loves you, like you are.

When you think about the price God paid for you, then you can say: "I must be important. I must have value."

You will begin to love God who loved you, and that will make you love others. When you do that, God is at work within you.

The Bible says: *You can do all things through Christ which strengthens you.*[Phil.4:13]

His strength in you is His love at work within you. And that is the greatest power on earth. *It is God who is at work in you, both to be willing, and to be doing His good pleasure.*Phil.2:13

## When You Value You

Because you have God's opinion of yourself, you no longer want to destroy the wonderful person God made. You value your body, your mind, your lungs, your organs, your blood, your heart. Since He accepts you, you accept yourself and you begin to accept others.

You speak for Him and salvation comes to people you talk to. You pray to Him and wonderful changes happen to people. You touch the sick and His wonderful power heals them.

Your body has become His temple. You are authorized to act on His behalf. You are part of God's plan to bless and heal and help and lift people.

Is it a sin to value what God values?

Has anyone the right to demean what God esteems?

When you realize that you are representing God, your whole value system and community outlook takes on quality.

You recognize that God is in you. God lives through you.

You cannot value or love or lift others until you

value and love yourself and are lifted by that self-value.

## What God Creates Is Remarkable

*All things were made by him and without him was not anything made.* Jn.1:3

All things include you. God created you.

> **Value what God created because His creations are perfect.**
>
> **Not to be what God has designed you to be is a waste.**

Strip away the cloak of pretension. Take away your labels, your profession, your reputation. Look deep inside yourself and see the picture of a human being made like God.

Value you and let God become, in and through you, all that He is. Then you become God in action. God will be living through you.

Learn to say:

I am here on God's behalf. I am made for God to live in and through. We are workers together. We share life together. We are winners. We are people lifters.

THE ONLY WAY Christ can reach out to hurting people is through me.

He has no hands but my hands.

This is why God values me and why I am vital to His love plan. ))))▶

## Chapter 9

# God Works Through You And Me

DURING THE SECOND world war, a beautiful statue of Jesus, in France, was badly damaged.

The villagers there loved their church and they affectionately gathered up the pieces of their broken statue of Jesus which stood in front of their church, and they repaired it.

Even the repair marks and broken lines reminded them of the scars of Christ's sufferings for them.

Every part of the statue was precious and they repaired it all—except the hands. They never found the hands.

Some of the people said, "What good is our Christ without hands?"

That gave someone an idea, and he had a bronze plaque attached to the statue engraved with these words: I have no hands but your hands!

One day a visitor saw the repaired statue of Christ, without hands, and wrote a poem:

> **I have no hands but your hands,
> to do my work today.**
>
> **I have no feet but your feet,
> to lead souls on the way.**
>
> **I have no tongue but your tongue,
> to tell them how I died.**
>
> **I have no help but your help,
> to bring them to God's side.**

The only way Christ can reach out His arms and lay His divine hands of blessing upon lives, is through those who have allowed Him to come home and to live in and through them.

You are His body now. His ministry in your community is expressed through you.

He longs to speak to souls about their salvation, and to convince them of the Gospel. And he can do it through you.

He wants to visit the lost, the sick, the prisoners, and to bless them. He can do it through you.

He will never send angels to do what He wants to do among people. He operates through you and me now. If we are too busy with other things, if we think we are not good enough, if we feel our own affairs are more important, if we think we do not have time, then our Christ is like that statue; He has no hands.

## God Never Gave Up on Us

This is why God values you and why He paid such a price to redeem you and to restore you to himself.

His original plan, when He created Adam and Eve in His own image, was for them to share His life, His plans, His work of love on this earth.

Sin entered the human race and separated us from God [Isa.59:1-2] and condemned us to death.[Rom. 6:23]

But God never gave up on us. He loved us too much to quit on us. So His Son, Jesus Christ, assumed all the judgment for all of our sins, in our place, and redeemed us and restored us to God, as though we had never sinned. You can now say:

It was love's idea to not let me die in my sins.

Jesus proved how much God values me.

He paid for me by giving His life in my place.

I am worth what God paid for me.

I shall never again condemn what God has paid so much to redeem.

I shall never put down what cost God so much to raise up.

When Dr. T.L. saw Jesus alive in a vision in 1948, the ministries of T.L. & Daisy and their entire family – for generations to come – were forever changed. The healing power of Christ and His resurrection LIFE is the Osborns' central message.

Raised on the platforms of global miracle evangelism, Osborn daughter Dr. LaDonna's worldwide ministry is also marked by supernatural healing miracles. Why? Because Jesus and His ministry are the same TODAY as in Bible days.

OSBORN CRUSADE – NIGERIA

OSBORN CRUSADE – INDONESIA

OSBORN CRUSADE – PHILIPPINES

OSBORN CRUSADE – COLOMBIA

OSBORN CRUSADE – TRINIDAD

OSBORN CRUSADE – ZAIRE

OSBORN CRUSADE – INDIA

OSBORN CRUSADE – PUERTO RICO

OSBORN CRUSADE – HOLLAND

Dr. LaDonna includes in her ministry the legacy of her mother (Dr. Daisy Washburn Osborn) by occasionally ministering especially to women. This Women's Conference in Nigeria encourages women in ministry from various nations of the world.

The spiritual landscape of nations around the world is being impacted by the rise of women who are proclaiming the GOOD NEWS of Jesus' love and healing power.

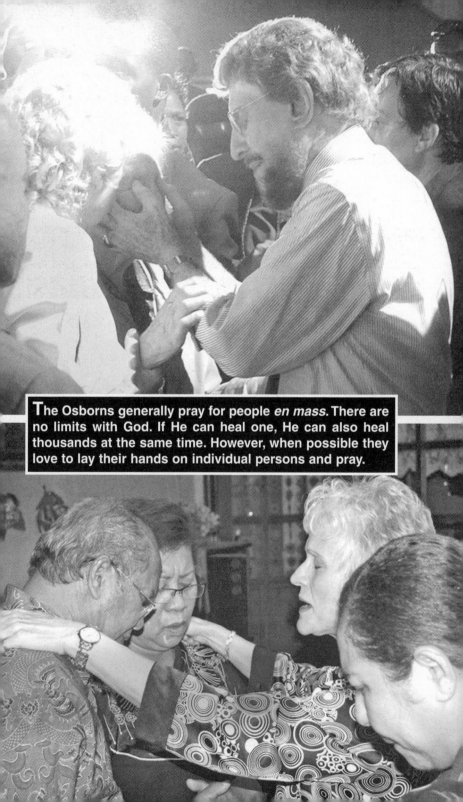

The Osborns generally pray for people *en mass*. There are no limits with God. If He can heal one, He can also heal thousands at the same time. However, when possible they love to lay their hands on individual persons and pray.

**T**ools for evangelism provided for soulwinning missions around the world has, for decades, been one of the proven outreaches of the Osborn Ministries. (T.L. and Daisy, at center)

The life and ministry of Dr. Daisy Washburn Osborn, wife of T.L., is unprecedented among Christian women in the church. Her positive example affected millions of women in over 70 nations, giving them true self-esteem in Christ.

**WOMEN'S MIRACLE DAY – UGANDA**

**WOMEN'S NATIONAL CONGRESS – E. AFRICA**

**AUSTRALIAN CONFERENCE**

**INDONESIAN WOMEN'S DAY – SURABAYA**

**WOMEN'S NATIONAL CONFERENCE – GHANA**

**SOUWINNING SEMINAR – NYANZA PROV.**

Over 100 beautiful gospel vans, loaded and equipped with tools for evangelism have been provided FREE for mission fields worldwide, by the Osborn Ministries.

OSBORN CRUSADE – Bogota

OSBORN CRUSADE – Accra

OSBORN TEACHING – Tulsa Campmeeting

OSBORN CRUSAD Nigeria

Hundreds of tape players – thousands of gospel tapes,

Huge airlifts of TONS of gospel literature and evangelism tools are provided free to national pastors, leaders and to missionaries overseas, for reaching the unreached with the message of God's love.

OSBORN CRUSADE – o

OSBORN CRUSADE – Kinshasa

OSBORN CRUSADE – W. Africa

OSBORN CRUSADE – Calabar

rovided free by Osborn Ministries.

**D**r. LaDonna Osborn has been involved with her parents in miracle evangelism from her youth. The same anointing that has rested upon T.L. and Daisy, is evident in LaDonna's own global ministry. As the gospel is proclaimed by either T.L. or LaDonna, crutches, canes, braces and wheelchairs are hoisted to signal miracles received through the power of God's word. As in Jesus' day, *The power of the Lord was present to heal.* Lu. 5:17

LaDonna and T.L. strategize global crusades and literature-distribution. Their preaching is always confirmed by miracles. TONS of their books seed church leaders and believers for spiritual harvests, impacting nations with Christ's gospel.

"What Christ's power and love have done for others, it will do in your life. This book contains the secrets of how to receive God's Best for YOU."
LaDonna and T.L. Osborn

Signs, wonders and miracles confirm the ministry of Dr. LaDonna as she promulgates the healing gospel in her global crusades.

**T.**L. and LaDonna are giving their BEST to reach nations with the gospel – often on *two fronts at once*.

**T.**L. Osborn proclaims the gospel to thousands in Lithuania where communism dominated since Lenin's Godless revolution. Today the new church is on the rise.

**D**r. LaDonna, in Beijing, dedicates tons of T.L.'s book, *"Healing the Sick"*, in Mandarin Chinese language.

**O**ne fifth of the world lives in China. *"Why should anyone hear the gospel twice before everyone has heard it once?"* We are seeding China NOW.

**O**sborn books in Mandarin, seeding for China's great soul harvest.

**C**hina has influenced the world for over 5,000 years. Now, the *old* is giving way to the *new*. God's LOVE and redemptive plan for humanity is the only hope for these millions.

# OSBORN MINISTRIES –

- Angola
- Argentina
- Armenia
- Australia
- Austria
- Azerbaijan
- Bangladesh
- Belarus
- Belgium
- Benin
- Bermuda
- Bolivia
- Botswana
- Brazil
- Bulgaria
- Burkina Faso
- Burundi

- Cambodia
- Cameroon
- Canada
- Central Afr. Rep.
- Chad
- Chile
- China
- Colombia
- Congo (Dem. Rep.)
- Congo (Rep.)
- Costa Rica
- Cuba
- Denmark
- Dominican Rep.
- Ecuador
- Egypt
- El Salvador
- England
- Estonia
- Ethiopia
- Finland
- France
- Gabon

- Georgia
- Germany
- Ghana
- Guatemala
- Haiti
- Honduras

LEGEND

Nations in which the Osborns
have proclaimed the Gospel
in face-to-face ministry.

- Hong Kong
- India
- Indonesia
- Ireland
- Italy
- Ivory Coast
- Jamaica
- Japan
- Kazakhstan
- Kenya
- Kyrgyzstan
- Laos
- Liberia
- Lithuania
- Luxemborg
- Madagascar
- Malawi
- Malaysia
- Mexico
- Mongolia
- Myanmar
- Netherlands

- New Zealand
- Nicaragua
- Nigeria
- Norway
- Pakistan
- Panama
- Papua N.Guinea
- Paraguay
- Peru
- Philippines
- Poland
- Portugal
- Puerto Rico
- Russia

- Rwanda
- Senegal
- South Africa
- South Korea
- Spain
- Sri Lanka
- Sweden
- Switzerland
- Taiwan
- Tajikistan
- Tanzania
- Thailand
- Togo
- Trinidad
- Uganda
- Ukraine
- United States
- Uruguay
- Uzbekistan
- Venezuela
- Vietnam
- Virgin Islands
- Zambia

"**P**artnership in this global ministry is miraculous. As we GO and REACH and LIFT and TOUCH people in Christ's name, you – our Partners – GO WITH US. It is YOUR ministry in action. PARTNERSHIP IS MINISTRY MULTIPLIED!"
– T.L. & LaDonna Osborn

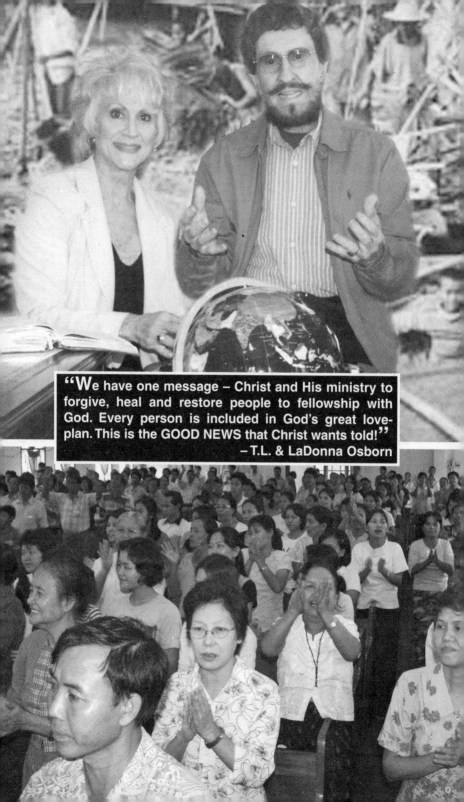

"**W**e have one message – Christ and His ministry to forgive, heal and restore people to fellowship with God. Every person is included in God's great love-plan. This is the GOOD NEWS that Christ wants told!"
– T.L. & LaDonna Osborn

Tens of thousands of weary Congolese gather to hear a message of hope from Dr. LaDonna. Thousands believe on and accept Jesus Christ after hearing the Gospel, and marvelous miracles of healing are witnessed daily.

**D**r. LaDonna Osborn is experiencing BIBLE DAYS in Point-Noire. *The blind receive their sight, and the lame walk ... the deaf hear ... and the poor have the Gospel preached to them.* Mat11:5

**D**r. LaDonna's lifetime involvement in mass miracle evangelism has equipped her to minister with ease and great authority, as shown here during the Osborn Festivals of Faith & Miracles in Kupang, Waingapu and Palangkaraya, Indonesia.

**LaDonna Osborn Gospel Seminar & Book Distribution**

LaDonna Osborn Festival of Faith & Miracles – Kupang, Indonesia

LaDonna Osborn Festival of Faith & Miracles – Waingapu, Indonesia

LaDonna Osborn Festival of Faith & Miracles – Palangkaraya, Indonesia

Waingapu, Indonesia

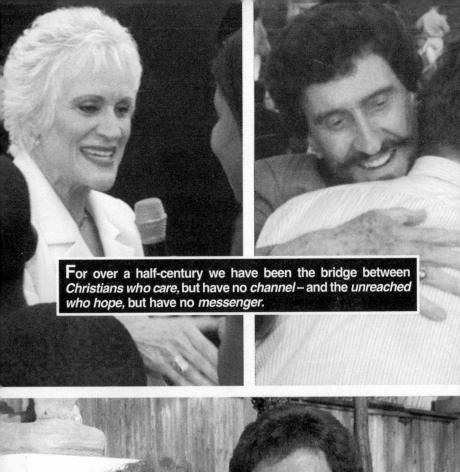

For over a half-century we have been the bridge between *Christians who care,* but have no *channel* – and the *unreached who hope,* but have no *messenger.*

We are thankful for believing Christians and leaders who choose us as their *Partners* in reaching the UNreached with the gospel. *Dr. T.L. Osborn* and daughter, *Dr. LaDonna Osborn*

The ministries of the Osborns have made an unprecedented impact on the world. They are considered by church leaders worldwide to be among the great soulwinners of our epoch. Dr. T.L. Osborn, Dr. Daisy Washburn Osborn (1924-1995) and Dr. LaDonna Osborn have ministered in over 100 nations.

I RECOGNIZE MY self-value, that God designed me for His lifestyle, and I now know that He considers me to be His best creation, and He ordained His best in life for me.

Whatever can be said about God, can be said about His offspring.

I am His child. I am in His family. ⟫➡

# Chapter 10

# Like Parent—Like Child

THE BIBLE SAYS: *So God created man in his own image. In the image of God created he him; male and female created he them.*[Gen.1:27]

God created human persons as much like himself as any child can be like its natural parents.

Later the Bible informs us that Adam and Eve bore a son, Seth.

The same words are used to describe Seth's resemblance to Adam, his father, as are used to describe your resemblance to God, your Father.

## In His Own Likeness

*Adam had a son in his own likeness, after his own image.*[Gen.5:3]

You see, whatever one can say about parents can be said of their offspring.

God planned that whatever could be said about Him, could be said about you.

The Bible explains the lifestyle and plan God designed for you and me.

God said, *Be fruitful and multiply, and replenish the earth, and subdue it; and have dominion over every living thing.*[Gen.1:28]

In Genesis 1:29-30 all of the possessions on earth that God gave to humankind are listed.

God never planned you or me for poverty, inferiority, sickness, depression, want or insecurity.

God never created anything inferior, not you, not me, not any human person.

As this powerful principle takes root in you, you begin to see and respect yourself as a member of divine royalty.

God's family is supposed to represent Him and to reflect His lifestyle on earth.

You ask, "What can I do about it?"

## Greatness Is Germinating in You

The first step is to recognize your value. When you do, you cause the seeds of greatness to germinate in you.

Those seeds will grow. It will be like a miracle at work in you.

You begin to think and feel and talk like someone of value, of dignity.

Your self-value commands respect.

Others treat you like you treat yourself.

They see you like you see yourself.

You merit the confidence of others when you practice trusting yourself.

> **You stamp your own value on your life by your very own thoughts, words and actions.**

Never entertain demeaning thoughts about yourself again. Never speak or act as a second class person.

MY HERITAGE IS to have God's best, to enjoy His companionship and to use His wealth and power for the good of myself and others.

God's love can never quit on me or anyone else.

Love never fails so I never lose.   ⟫➡

# Chapter 11

# Wonderful People Lifters

JESUS SAID, *I was hungry and you gave me meat: I was thirsty and you gave me drink: I was a stranger and you took me in: Naked, and you clothed me: I was sick and you visited me: I was in prison and you came to me.*Mat.25:35-36

Then He said: *Anytime you did this for one of the least of these, you have done it to me.*Mat.25:40

If we want to really discover Jesus Christ, we will find Him in the prisons, among the sick, the naked, the needy. We discover Christ and serve Him as we serve them.

## The Ex-Prostitute

A young woman was converted in New York City and she became a great soulwinner. She had been addicted to narcotics and was a prostitute. She lost an arm in a fight and wears a prosthesis.

Following her conversion, she believed in God's value of her life. Though an ex-prostitute and physically disabled, she believed she was vital to God's love plan.

She understood that Jesus wanted to reach out and touch and love and save and heal and bless other prostitutes and unchurched people. She realized that He wanted to do that through her, that she was now His body. He had come to live in her and now He would heal and love and lift people through her as she acted in His name.

She wanted to find a way to reach out to needy, hurting people like she had been. She turned every stone to find a way to help them.

Finally she had a terrific idea.

## The Porno Theatre

There were three pornographic cinemas, side by side, in a certain area of a New York City ghetto. The middle one was for sale.

That young lady never stopped until she, and others working with her, managed to raise enough money to buy that ex-porno theatre. They began having gospel meetings there where the need was so urgent.

Opposite the entrance of that converted theatre, there were three hotels, dominated by pimps and their prostitutes.

That young woman, a regenerated prostitute and ex-narcotic addict, chose that very place to go to work for God.

She had God's viewpoint. She knew she could only love and serve God by loving and serving those who were hurting, who were forgotten and unloved, those who were unchurched.

Today several hundred people attend church there. Instead of condemning the social cancer in that ghetto, that group of soulwinners moved in and started curing that cancer. They demonstrated true Christian faith in action and God's true value system of people.

You see that is the only way to really discover true faith in God.

---

**What you do to others, you do to Christ. Faith is not discovered in beautiful words in a sanctuary, but in beautiful deeds and actions out among people who are in need.**

---

## No One Is Hopeless

When we discover God's value system, we never see a human person as being hopeless.

To say that anyone is hopeless is to say, God does not care about him or her.

To say, God does not care, means we do not care, because He can only care through us.

He does care. He loves people. He cares through us. And His love can never quit.

The scars of His love for us prove His value of us, and of everyone else, regardless of how anyone looks or lives.

## Nobodies Turned Somebodies

I heard a young pastor of one of America's large churches say, "Nine years ago we went into this city with nothing. We did not expect people to come to us. We chose to go to them like Jesus did."

He said, "We never left the area for eighteen months. Every day, from morning until night, my wife and I knocked on doors, visited prisons, ministered in hospitals and houses and got people saved out where they live and work and suffer and die."

That pastor said, "We went to the people who had problems."

After nine years, over two thousand people attend each service at that church.

Many formerly destitute families, ex-prostitutes, prisoners and drunkards, are today owners of businesses and are productive citizens.

They have produced a small army of inspired Christians who are soulwinners. They have discovered God's value system of people.

Senators, doctors and lawyers attend that church now, and it is a powerful instrument for God's work.

That pastor has discovered the vital principle in life. He has discovered that in serving those who are hungry and thirsty, the orphans, the prisoners, the naked, the sick and the suffering, he is actually serving Christ.

## God's Value System

The Bible says, *Faith works by love.*[Gal.5:6]

John asks: *If you do not love someone whom you have seen, how can you love God whom you have not seen?* [1Jn.4:20]

So to love God is to love others. *Let us not love in word, neither in tongue,* [as John said,] *but in deed and in truth.*[1Jn.3:18]

John asks: How can we talk about loving God, or serving God, or expressing our faith in God, if we know people are in need and do nothing about it? [1Jn.3:17]

We only discover real faith as we act in real love toward others. Jesus is wherever there are people in need. The way we respond to them, is the way we respond to Him.

The whole principle is getting God's view of people, accepting His value of human beings.

God wants you to discover the essential fact that every human person is created by Him, for His lifestyle, to fulfill His purpose on this earth — and every person includes you.

To discover that principle puts your own life into perspective. It gives dignity, purpose and value to living. It lifts you to the level of royalty, of nobility, of self-value.

# WONDERFUL PEOPLE LIFTERS

THE STRONGER GOD can be in me, the more He can lift others through me.

I am God's starting point.

My life is the very breath of God.

His life in me means His love is in me.

God is at work in me.　　　　　)))➡

## Chapter 12

# Never Demean—Always Esteem

KEEP THE PICTURE of God's kind of being in your mind. Self-value and self-esteem are the noblest garments you can wear.

Purpose to never discredit the **you** that God values so much.

Determine to never demean the **you** that God created in His own image.

Everything from God is channeled through you. The stronger God can be in you, the more He can lift others through you.

### God Takes Hold with Your Hands

The more love that fills you, the more love you will discover being expressed through you.

Poor people cannot help poor people.

Down people cannot lift down people.

Only happy people can make others happy.

Only positive people can make others positive.

## You are God's starting point.

The greatest possible achievement in life is to be the terrific person God created you to be.

To disregard that noble purpose results in frustration, unhappiness and deterioration.

The reason there is so much loneliness, depression, drug and sex abuse, insecurity and even suicide, is because people do not value themselves.

They see themselves as a speck in the universe, a number in a computer, of no personal significance. They look into their mirror and feel unimportant, helpless, hopeless.

### When God Lives in You

But when you discover your value as a creation of God, to represent Him, your life takes on purpose, a reason for being. You suddenly realize:

* I am made for success. I was not put here to stand in a social aid line, to feel shame, to be lonely.

* God and I can walk together. We can change our world.

You look in the mirror as a new day dawns, and you no longer see a despondent, rejected and downcast nobody. You see God's creation in human flesh.

You say:

"Good morning, God. I see your handiwork in me. I am masterfully made, created to be your partner.

"God, You look great in me this morning. What good and productive things are You and I up to today?"

To succeed with purpose and to get life's best, it is vital that you:

> **Recognize your own self-value.**
>
> **Understand your potential.**

## Discover Your Treasures

You are like Columbus gazing at the new world he had discovered. There are valuable treasures to be uncovered and developed. They will turn you into a successful, happy, healthy and productive achiever, and countless others will share in the benefits.

Your thinking is like electricity that can be captured, harnessed and channeled into creative productivity for yourself and for the good of others.

The most powerful concept you can hold is that God is in you. Your life is the very breath of God.

God's life in you means His love is in you, limitless, healing, lifting, blessing you and others through you.

I HAVE OPENED my doors, my heart and my ears to others. I can never be lonely again.

I learn by teaching.

I gain by listening.

I reap by planting.

I receive by giving. ⠀⠀⠀⠀⠀⠀)⠀⠀➡

# Chapter 13

# Sharing God's Lifestyle

**W**HEN YOU DISCOVER the price God paid for you, then you discover the true value of every human person. You begin to realize that God paid for you so that He can come home to you and live in you, as He originally designed you for. He lives in you in order to share in and through you His lifestyle with others.

* We are saved to save others.

* We are lifted to lift others.

* We are blessed to bless others.

The Bible says: *Whatever you sow, you shall reap.* Gal.6:7

* Whatever you plant, you will harvest.

* When you sow love and kindness, that is what you reap.

* If you sow judgment and condemnation, you will be judged and condemned by people.

* If you are merciful, you will reap mercy.Mat.5:7

The kind of seed you sow in others is the kind of life you will reap for yourself.

This principle has lifted everyone who ever discovered it.

It is God's value system.

## What Produces Millionaires

God's value system is captured in these lines for the benefit of anyone who wishes to succeed in life:

Find a need and meet it.

Find a hurt and heal it.

Find a desire and fill it.

Find a problem and solve it.

These lines express the principle that has produced millionaires.

You can discover this principle, and apply it in life, when you discover that each human person, including yourself, has infinite value to God.

Knowing that fact and realizing the price Jesus Christ paid to redeem each human person to God, you discover the principle of blessing yourself by blessing others, of experiencing healing in your own life as you share healing with others in need.

## Never Be Lonely

That is why we say that you can only succeed as you help others succeed.

Jesus said, *Give and it shall be given to you; good measure, pressed down, and shaken together and run-*

*ning over, shall others give to you.*[Lu.6:38] He means whatever you give, more of it shall be given to you.

Jesus' rule was: *All things that you want people to do to you, do those things to them.*[Mat.7:12] This means: Whatever you do to others you will reap from others.

Jesus said that we are to be seed planters. He said: *The seed is the word.*[Lu.8:11] And *the field is the world*[Mat.13:38] — the world of people around us.

Plant kindness in people and you will reap kindness. Heal people by planting seeds of love and you will reap healing love from others.

Hate people and you will be hated. Envy people and you will be envied.

Open your door, your heart and your ears to others, and you will never be lonely. You will do this when you discover God's value system of people.

## Showing What We Are

Jesus showed us God at work in Him by what He did for others. We show our Christ at work in us by what we do for others.

When we value people like God values them,

* We will heal them rather than bruise them.
* We will lift them rather than put them down.
* We will esteem them rather than demean them.
* We will forgive them rather than judge them.

Jesus showed us God by what happened to people who came in contact with Him. We show what God is like in our lives by what happens to people who come in contact with us.

You grow as you help others grow. You prosper as you help others prosper.

You learn by teaching. You gain by listening. You reap by planting. You receive by giving.

A dynamic change takes place in your life when you discover God, at home again in you, sharing His lifestyle and His abundance with other lives, through you.

You discover God at work in you, carrying out His big kingdom business through you.

He values everyone. He proved it by what He paid for each one. He works through you showing His love and His value of people. You discover that He is manifested through you and that gives your life value.

## When Love Is Real Love

The songwriter said:

*A bell is not a bell 'til you ring it;*

*A song is not a song 'til you sing it.*

*Love in your heart is not put there to stay;*

*Love is not love 'til you give it away.*

So take a new look at others today. *Lift up your eyes and look on the fields.*Jn.4:35

It is as you reach out to others that God reaches out through you and to you. It is when you bless others that God blesses you. So think of that when you look at other people.

Plant in them what you want to reap in your own life. You are the master of your own harvest. Just plant in others the kind of seed you want to reap, and God will fulfill your greatest dreams.

Learning this, you are discovering the greatest principle of life, the principle that guarantees you peace, happiness, success and fulfillment.

I RECOGNIZE MY ROOTS in God. My life is His life in human flesh.

I know God values me and has paid for me.

I esteem what He values.

I have had a rebirth of my self-worth.   )))➡

# Chapter 14

# Rebirth Of Self-Worth

GOD'S LIFE IN YOU means that His power is there in you, immeasurable, miraculous, positive, productive, and flowing out to others through you.

You need never feel abandoned or alone, guilty or condemned.

You need never feel inferior or without value, confused or without purpose, afraid or anxious.

When you recognize your roots in God and see yourself as His intended habitation; when you discover how easy it is to experience God in you, you will actually have a *rebirth of self-worth*.

Your very life becomes the miracle of God's life breathed into you.

## Basis for Enthusiasm

People begin to respect you and to draw strength and inspiration from you. This is because you have discovered self-respect, self-value, self-esteem which is the basis for a positive, enthusiastic outlook on life.

You begin to think and talk like those who trusted God in Bible days.

I have paraphrased for you some of the powerful statements in Psalms 91:

*God is my refuge and strength. He delivers me from every snare and pestilence.*

*He covers me. His truth is my armor. I am not afraid, day or night. Though tragedy strikes all around me, my security is in God. Nothing destroys Him and He lives in me.*

*No evil befalls me. No plague comes to my dwelling because God is there. His angels keep charge over me wherever I go. They even bear me up above any danger that is in my way.*

*I am able to walk right over any enemy that intends to injure or destroy me.*

*These blessings are because God has set His love upon me and I have set my love upon Him. He knows my name and sets me in a high place.*

*When I call upon Him, He answers me. He is with me in trouble. He delivers me and honors me. He satisfies me with long life and shows me His salvation.*

## Created for Dignity and Nobility

The human person is the only creation on this earth that yearns for self-respect, self-value, self-esteem.

People made in God's image cannot tolerate life without dignity. They will withdraw into rooms and close the blinds. They will shut themselves away from society, or will lay down in ditches or gutters and gradually die, the victims of lonely and purposeless abandonment.

The curse of resignation, the cancer of futility and abandonment only develop in people who fail to discover their self-value, their dignity, their potential for happy prosperous living.

## Born for Greatness

You are born for greatness, not mediocrity. You are created for health, not for sickness. You are here for success, not for failure.

You are created for abundance and happiness, not for poverty and disappointment.

You are designed for esteem, dignity and accomplishment, not for shame, abuse and bankruptcy.

You will actually have a *rebirth of self-worth*.

You will be poised instead of tense.

Confident instead of fearful.

Directed rather than confused.

Bold rather than timid.

Enthusiastic instead of depressed.

Energetic rather than tired or bored.

Self-forgiving rather than self-condemning.

## Manifesting God in Human Form

When you discover that God is in you, around you, under you, with you; when you accept the fact that you came from Him and are made like Him; then you become the God person you were designed to be.

You actually become the manifestation of God.

Your desires are the expression of His desires through you.

Your ambitions become the result of His ambitions within you.

You become a living miracle with power at work in and through you.

You become God in action.

You discover your God-like value.

You begin to think, talk and act like **somebody.**

As you discover your self-value and learn to esteem and appreciate yourself because of God living in you, you become a positive, uplifting influence in your own home, community and in your world.

How could you ever again be negative or downcast when there is so much evidence that you are created as a God being?

# REBIRTH OF SELF-WORTH

I AM MADE by God.
His best material is in me.
I am the product of love.
I am created for greatness.
I am God's best. ⟫➡

# Chapter 15

# The Master Artist

IT IS SAID that Michelangelo started sculpting at least forty-four great statues in solid marble. But to our knowledge, he only finished fourteen of them, such as the enormous statue of David in Florence, Italy, the Pieta in Rome's basilica, and his monumental Moses. I have gazed in awe at these renowned *chefs-d'œuvre*.

Just think. At least thirty great works of art which were conceived and partially sculptured by the great master artist, were left unfinished. (Fortunately, the huge chunks of partially worked marble are preserved in an Italian museum.)

Some show only a hand or a leg or an elbow and shoulder or a foot with toes. The total design in the great master artist's mind was never executed.

The rest of the body remains frozen in solid marble, locked up forever, never to be formed into the great Michelangelo's total design.

For some reason God who formed you in His likeness, has purposed that this shall not be your case. He has marked you and caused this book to come into your hands because He has purposed that you are one of His best, and He wills that you discover the principle of your value.

## You Are God's Best

The material in you is the best. You are redeemed. The full price has been paid. You are pure marble, a pure human person designed and created by God, in His own image, with absolutely unlimited potential existing inside of you. It is all there.

God sees in you the wonder and marvel that He envisaged when He formed you in His likeness.

The Master Sculptor is reaching out to you, through this book, to touch you with His miracle power, to make you a full, wonderful and perfect expression for Him to reveal His power through. All of His value is in you.

The only way His full potential in you will not be developed is if you fail to see your value and position with Him.

He is the Master Sculptor. You are His material.

When you demean yourself, condemn and negate yourself, you are the one who limits what the Master can produce in you.

**When you say NO,** I am not worthy, I am no good, I am incapable, I am inferior, you tie the Master's hands and your life is like one of those unfinished chunks of marble left by Michelangelo with only a head or leg or arm completed.

**When you say YES,** the Creator is released in you to develop your finest potential, to create you as His masterpiece.

---

### Grasp God's Viewpoint

**Yield to His full development.**

**Believe in the full potential of God at work in you.**

**You are His best.**

---

## Tragedy or Triumph

**The greatest tragedy** in your life would be for you to live and die and never come out of yourself—to never realize the possibilities hidden within you.

Discover this principle and resolve that such shall never be the case in your life.

**The greatest triumph** in life is to discover yourself in Christ, to discover the rich, full happy life He created you for, then to develop that unlimited life by sowing it in others and reaping God's abundant lifestyle of total peace, happiness, success and fulfillment.

I AM...
As young as my dreams,
As young as my new ideas,
As young as my new values.
There is no age limit for God's ability in me.
I accept God's value of me.　　　　)))➡

# Chapter 16

# Accepting God's Value

Now IT IS time to let the Master know, by your action, that you accept His new value system for your life and for the lives of others.

What can you do? Not much.

* Just confess what you believe.
* Confess that His new dreams and ideas and concepts and values have set the standard for your new life plan.
* Then purpose to do something about these principles.

## Your Faith—Your Ministry

Paul covered the entire principle of conversion in two simple steps:

1) *If you believe in your heart that God raised Jesus from the dead, and—*

2) *If you confess with your mouth that He is your Lord,—*

*you shall be saved.*Rom.10:9

That is the principle of receiving any blessing from God.

First: Believe it in your heart. That is **your faith.**

Second: Confess it with your mouth to others. Share it with others. Give it to others. That is **your ministry.**

This is one of the greatest moments of your life.

You may be young, and you want to be part of God's plan in life. You will never be the same again.

Older people can turn around too and begin a brand new positive useful life. It is never too late when you have had a new vision.

David Ben Gurion, founder of the State of Israel, learned French after he was seventy.

The great painter, Titian, was painting masterpieces when he was ninety-eight years old.

You are as young as your dreams, as your new projects, new ideas and new values.

## No Age Limit for God's Ability

An old man, ninety-four years old, came in a wheelchair to visit Daisy and me in Tulsa. He held meetings in the jail every week and had already won over a hundred souls to Jesus Christ.

Do you know what he wanted? A projector and a set of our documentary crusade films which contain my messages as they were preached, our prayers for the unconverted and for the sick and the miracles which took place among the people who received Christ. Our DocuMiracle films have been used globally in evangelism and church planting activities. Today they are available on DVD. See www.osborn.org for more information.

That elderly gentleman was going to travel across America to show those documentary films and tell the people about Jesus. He was not a preacher, but he had God's idea about life and he realized how much God values each individual, how much a person is worth to God.

He said to us:

> **"I cannot die! I cannot die! I have too much to do. Too many people are lost and need Jesus, and I have to tell them."**

He was ninety-four years old but he had no time to die. What a beautiful example of getting God's attitude about life and of perceiving His value system.

You see, no one is too old and no one is too young.

I was saved at the age of twelve.

I became a preacher at the age of fifteen.

I was married at the age of eighteen. I was a missionary in India at the age of twenty-one.

No one is too young. No one is too old. Today is your day and God has caused this book to come into your hands to encourage you to discover this vital principle of *your infinite value to God and to people.*

The miracle you need is beginning to take form in your life because you are *seeing yourself as God sees you.*

# ACCEPTING GOD'S VALUE

I WELCOME GOD'S love voice.

He reminds me...

Of my divine origin,

Of my high purpose,

Of my infinite value,

Of His love plan to help me achieve, enjoy and share His best in life. ))))▶

# Chapter 17

# Redeemed From Inferiority

FOR THOUSANDS OF YEARS, the way to God's blessings in life has been defined clearly in the Bible, but human beings do not always accept those beautiful ideas because of religious prejudice.

The barrage of conflicting religious doctrines frighten people away from God.

Humanism has tried for centuries to make a more attractive appeal based on logistics and reason. Seeking to placate the conscience of people, they cry: "Humankind is good."

Traditional religious orators say, "No. We must stress the basic fact that humankind is bad."

## God Is Good! I Can Be Good!

Both arguments miss the point because they focus attention upon the human person in itself.

Rather than to argue either that people are bad or that people are good, the positive option transcends all human assessment and builds on the foundation that **God is good.**

If God is good, you can be good. Since He created you in His own image and likeness, you can have dignity and self-value.

> # One can never exalt God by demeaning His offspring.

I have been criticized because I do not stand before audiences and expose or assail or condemn the sins of people.

A human person who has not found the way to God, is already conscious of guilt and condemnation.

## He Loved You All the Time

I choose to point you to God who is good. He loves you in whatever state you may be, so much that He paid the supreme price of giving His own Son, Jesus, to redeem you from all sin by suffering the penalty for your sin, in your place, and He did it before you ever knew you needed it.

Since He loved you that much, even when you were oblivious to His goodness, that gives you reason to believe that you have divine value and dignity.

Whether you are basically good (as the humanists and psychologists say), or bad (as the priests, rabbis and preachers say), really does not matter. Without God, you are not normal. You are not living up to your potential.

## You Were Made for Life

Life, as God designed it for you, is too valuable for you to miss. There is too much for you to be, to have, to enjoy, to do. To resign or to surrender hope is to sin, to deteriorate, to die.

You are made for life. That is why this book is in your hand.

God created you for greatness, for success, for health, for happiness and for fulfillment.

Look beyond any facade or mask, and look deep within your heart where you yearn for God's life-style. It is there, deep within you.

So welcome the voice of love that does not attack and condemn you, but that honestly gives you hope by reminding you that God is there, loving, caring.

## Welcome God's Love Voice

Welcome the love message of the gospel that tells you that God created you to be exactly like Him; that your purpose is to be Him in action; that He so valued you that He paid the infinite price to redeem you from inferiority, deterioration and sin.

Once you understand this and accept it, God can share His life in and through you.

He is unchanging, unbeatable, unlimited.

You can become all that God is.

God is the same when He lives in and through you. God does not change inside of you.

Once you have accepted God's love plan and have received Jesus Christ into your life:

* You become God in the flesh again.
* You become the expression of God among people.
* You become love in action.
* You become good because God in you is good.
* You experience power, God's power.

You may be overwhelmed by this information. You may have thought you were a nobody.

But God's love voice encourages you to look beyond your humanity to His love plan and to see that all of the time that you were in shame, God kept right on loving you, because He created you to live in. And though you sinned against Him, His love caused Him to find a way to save you and restore you to Him. The price He paid is the proof of what He believes you are worth.

Perhaps you never heard anyone tell you that you are so valuable to God that He gave His Son to pay for you.

Your conscience has condemned you. Sermon-izers have threatened and frightened you. Your own habits and lifestyle have undermined you. You may be alone, afraid, guilty.

## Now God Speaks

Now this love voice of God is lifting you up to Him by reminding you of your origin in Him, of your design for success, of God's love plan to re-deem you, so that you can enjoy the abundant life you were created for.

Look beyond yourself, and see God. Discover your dignity and self-value. Let your heart leap with new hope. Say:

**I want to let God in. I am created for great-ness. I respond to this gentle love voice that brings me good news and reminds me that I am God's best. This is the good life I am made for. This is the way to God's best in life!**

**I am not worthless. God thinks I am worth everything He paid to redeem me. He gives me dignity and self-esteem because He created me.**

**I am thankful. I am somebody. I understand now, why it was necessary for me to discover this vital principle of God's value system for my life.**

# YOU ARE GOD'S BEST

# My Value...

### ( In 60 Seconds )

**I** AM VALUABLE because I am created in **God's class of being.**

**I** am VITAL because **God's plan involves me.**

**M**y HERITAGE is **to have God's best,** to enjoy **His companionship** and to **use His wealth and power** for the good of myself and others.

**I** am CREATED for **life, love, power, prosperity, success** and **dignity.**

**T**he SEEDS OF GREATNESS **are in me.** God never created me to be a **"Nobody,"** but a real **"SOMEBODY."**

**I** therefore **recognize my SELF-VALUE,** that God designed me **for His lifestyle** and I now know that **He planned Life's BEST for me as His child.**

**I** shall no longer **discredit** or **demean** or **destroy** what God created in His own image and **values so much.**

**I** welcome **God's friendly voice.** He reminds me of my **divine origin,** of my **high purpose,** and of **His Love-Plan** to help me **achieve, enjoy** and **share HIS BEST** in life.

Dr. T.L. Osborn

I HAVE HEARD God's voice of love.

I welcome His life in me.

Never again will I destroy what God values.

I am accepted.

I see myself in God's image. We are at peace. ⟫➤

# Chapter 18

# Tell God What You've Discovered

I INVITE YOU now to allow the Master Artist to finish sculpting you until your finest potential is discovered.

See yourself as God sees you. See the unlimited possibilities that beckon you.

**You are part of a winning team.** Nothing can stop you and God together.

Tell God that you have decided to be part of His plan, to accept His value of yourself, to welcome Him home to live in and through you.

Say this to God:

> **Oh Lord, I have heard Your love voice through this book which You caused to come to my hands.**
>
> **I believe that You have spoken to me through this book and I want to be what You want me to be.**
>
> **I have discovered Your new value system in life. I have learned what a price You paid to prove how You value me. The life of Your**

Son was sacrificed and His blood was shed to make me clean.[Rom.5:8,9]

I believe in You, Lord. I receive Your new life. Thank You for valuing me too much to let me die in my sins. Thank You for the power that makes me a new creature, now that I have welcomed You home to live in me.

The blood of Jesus Christ cleanses me.[1Jn.1:7] His life regenerates me. [1Pet.1:23] The joy of Christ fills me.[Jn.15:11;16:24]

I am of infinite value.[1Pet.1:7] Thank You that You love me. I am Yours.[Jn.6:37]

You have made my body Your temple. I am redeemed and accepted. I am commissioned in the kingdom to represent You in this life.[1Cor.6:19,20]

I am as valuable to You as anyone. I am as beautiful in Your eyes as anyone. I have Your nature. I am loved. I can love others. Whatever I sow in others, I will reap.[Gal.6:8]

Thank You that I am part of Your plan. I have a place no one else can fill.[Eph.2:10]

No longer will I condemn myself nor will I ever again destroy what You value.[Ac.10:15]

Now I am accepted. I can do Your work. I am born again. I am a new creature. I have repented of my old values. I have changed my mind about myself and about other people.

Knowing how You value a human life has given me a new value of human persons.

I see you, Lord, with new eyes. I see others, as You see them. I see myself in Your image.

Together we can never fail. Father, everything is possible for You.[Mk.14:36] Thank You, Lord that You now live in me.

In Jesus' name.

Amen.

# YOU ARE GOD'S BEST

# THE *MISSION*
# OF CHRISTIANITY

## *OSBORN MINISTRY REVIEW*

---

**T**HE GLOBAL MISSION of Christianity is to witness of Christ and of His resurrection to *the entire world* – to *every creature.*[Mk.16:15]

---

The Apostle Paul said, *Whoever shall call on the name of the Lord shall be saved.*[Rom.10:13]

T.L. and Daisy Osborn shared a worldwide ministry together for over five decades, before her demise in 1995. T.L. resolved to continue his global ministry to multitudes.

The Osborn daughter, Dr. LaDonna, assumed a prominent role in the leadership of the Osborn world ministry. As the fame of her preaching ministry spread, she continued being involved in trans-evangelical seminars and mass miracle crusades in new fields of the world such as *Russia*, nations of *French-speaking Africa, Eurasia* and the world's most populous nation, *China.*

As CEO of *OSBORN Ministries Int'l.*, LaDonna's expertise is making possible the expansion of this ministry in nations around the world. Learn more about the Osborn Global Outreaches through their website, *www.osborn.org.*

The Osborns have reached millions for Christ in over a hundred nations during more than six decades. This ministry-brief is included here to inspire young believers that they, too, can carry the *gospel torch into all the world.*[Mk.16:15]

## Mass Miracle Evangelism

Tommy Lee Osborn and Daisy Marie Washburn were married in Los Banos, California in 1942, at the ages of 17 and 18. In 1945 they went to India as missionaries but were unable to convince the people of these ancient religions—Muslims and Hindus —about Christ. They had not yet discovered the truths about miracles. They returned to the USA dismayed and disheartened—but not dissuaded.

Soon after their demoralizing return home, the Lord appeared to them both, at different times, as they searched for the answer to their dilemma.

* They began to discover the Bible truths that create faith for biblical miracles.

* They had learned in India that for people of non-Christian nations to believe the gospel, they must witness miracle proof that Jesus Christ is alive today.

* They discovered that signs, miracles and wonders are essential to convincing *non*-Christian nations about the gospel.

> Jesus was...***approved of God*** *among people by **miracles** and **wonders** and **signs**, which God did by Him in the midst of the people.*[Ac.2:22]

These dynamic truths created in their spirits fresh faith in God's Word. With this new lease on life and having discovered the scriptural facts about miracles, they *re*-launched their soulwinning saga in 1949—this time in the Caribbean island-nation of Jamaica.

During thirteen weeks of ministry there, hundreds of biblical miracles confirmed their preaching.

* Over a hundred deaf-mutes were healed;

* Over ninety totally blind people received sight;

* Hundreds of crippled, paralyzed and lame people were restored;

* Most important of all, *nearly ten thousand souls received Jesus Christ as their Savior.*

That success motivated their new global ministry, proclaiming the gospel to multitudes. In the era when so-called *"Third World"* nations were mostly *colonized* by European governments, the Osborns pioneered the concept of *Mass Miracle Evangelism.* Such methods had not been witnessed since the epoch of the Early Church. T.L. and Daisy addressed audiences of tens of thousands throughout the dangerous years of *nationalism* when foreign political domination was being repulsed by the awakening *"Third World"* nations.

Their example inspired national men and women, globally, to arise from their restrictive past, and to become leading gospel messengers and church builders in the unevangelized nations of the world. Many of them are numbered among the most distinguished and successful Christian leaders today.

The largest churches in the world are no longer in America or Europe. They are being raised up by anointed and talented national pastors. Single churches in Africa seat 50,000 plus people under one roof. To God be the glory.

## Global Evangelism Concepts

During T.L. and Daisy's unprecedented years as an evangelism team, they inaugurated numerous programs to reach the unreached. Their concept of *National Missionary Assistance* resulted in them sponsoring over 30,000 national preachers as full time missionaries to unevangelized tribes and villages where new, self-supporting churches became established globally.

The Osborn literature is published in more than 130 languages. Their DocuMiracle crusade films, audio and video CDs and DVDs, and their digital productions (including Bible courses), are produced in over 70 languages and are circulated around the world.

They have provided airlifts and huge shipments of literature and of soulwinning tools for gospel ministries abroad. They have furnished scores of four-wheel drive vehicles equipped with films, projectors, screens, generators, public-address systems, audio cassettes and cassette players, plus literature for reaching the unreached.

## Publishing The Gospel

Dr. Daisy's five major books are *pacesetters* in Christian literature for women — *unique examples of **inclusive** language that consistently addresses both genders.*

T.L. has authored over 20 major books. He wrote his first, HEALING THE SICK, during their mission to Jamaica in 1950. Now in its 46th edition, it is a global favorite, used as a Bible School text book in many nations.

The publisher calls HEALING THE SICK *A Living Classic* — a faith-building best-seller since 1950. Over a million copies are in print, circulating healing truth throughout the world.

## Their Global Saga

In T.L.'s ninth decade of life, the Osborn ministry continues to expand. Following Daisy's demise, T.L. has continued his global evangelism crusades, and his daughter, Dr. La Donna, has expanded her ministries of evangelism and of church leadership to nearly every continent as she carries the *torch of the gospel* into this century's new frontiers.

Like the Apostle Paul, LaDonna says:

> *I am not ashamed of the gospel of Christ, for it is the power of God to salvation to everyone who believes.* Rom.1:16

She believes that:

*The World is the **Heart** of the Church,* and *The Church is the **Hope** of the World.*

She contends that:

Without the *World*, the *Church is **meaningless*** and Without the *Church*, the *World is **hopeless***.

## Colonialism
## Nationalism
## Globalism/Evangelism

Dr. LaDonna Osborn knows the ministry of World Evangelism. Since childhood, she has lived on the front lines of global SOULWINNING—from the days of *colonialism*, through the turbulent years of *nationalism*, and into this century of *globalism*, *mass evangelism* and *national* and *international Church growth*.

The Osborns hold forth these simple truths:

1) That the Bible is as valid today as it ever was;

2) That the divine calling for every believer is to witness of Christ to the unconverted;

3) That every soul won to Christ can become His representative; and

4) That miracles, signs and wonders are what distinguish Christianity from being just another philosophical religion.

To demonstrate these biblical issues is the essence of the global *MISSION of Christianity.*

Just as with the Apostle Paul, Dr. LaDonna and Dr. T.L. state:

> *The ministry we have received of the Lord is to testify to the gospel of the grace of God;* [Ac.20:24] *to preach the gospel in the regions beyond.*[2Cor.10:16]

Their partial testimony is recorded for posterity in their 512 page unique pictorial, THE GOSPEL ACCORDING TO T.L. AND DAISY.

The history of the Osborn ministry is also recorded in their unique and historical 24-volume *Encyclo-Biographical Anthology*. It contains more than 23,000 pages, 30,946 photos, 636 *Faith Digest* magazines, 2,024 pages of personal, hand-written diary notes, 1,011 pages of Osborns' news letters, 1,062 pages of unpublished historical data about their world ministry, 2,516 world mission reports, and 6,113 Christian ministry reports.

These 24 giant tomes span over six feet of shelf space and have taken their place in the archives and libraries of institutions of higher learning around the world, including such renowned universities and libraries as: University of Cambridge, Cambridge, England; University of Oxford, Oxford, England; Asbury Theological Seminary, Wilmore, USA; British Library, London, England; Central Bible College, Springfield, USA; Christ for the Nations, Dallas, USA; Fuller Theological Seminary, Pasadena, USA; Messenger College, Joplin, USA; National Library, Sofia, Bulgaria; ORU, Tulsa, USA; Ramkhamhaeng University, Bangkok, Thailand; Regent University, Virginia Beach, USA; Universidad Interamericana de Puerto Rico, Ponce, Puerto Rico; Université de Cocody, Abidjan, Ivory Coast; University of Ghana, Legon-Accra, Ghana; Université de Kinshasa, Kinshasa, Democratic Republic of the Congo; Université de Lomé, Lomé, Togo; University of Nairobi, Nairobi, Kenya; University of Maseno, Maseno, Kenya; Université Marien Ngouabi, Brazzaville, Congo; Université Omar Bongo, Libreville, Gabon; University of Wales, Bangor, Wales; Vernadsky National Library, Kiev, Ukraine; Word of Life, Uppsala, Sweden; (plus many more), and the archives of many leading denominational headquarters.